ABOVE NEW YORK

by
ROBERT CAMERON

A COLLECTION OF HISTORICAL
AND ORIGINAL AERIAL
PHOTOGRAPHS OF NEW YORK CITY

with introduction by
GEORGE PLIMPTON

and text by
PAUL GOLDBERGER

Cameron and Company, San Francisco, California

ORCHARD BEACH AND CITY ISLAND *(opposite)*   *text on page 160*   CONEY ISLAND

ST. PATRICK'S 1922

text on page 160

SAINT PATRICK'S CATHEDRAL *(opposite)*

TABLE OF CONTENTS

Such a book as this does not reach publication without more than the usual amount of cooperation
from many people. So, for their encouragement and expertise, I thank the following:

Merijane Block, Robert Burger, Cornell Capa, Phoebe Cameron, Todd Cameron, Robert Evans, Christopher Gray, Nina Gray, Sidney Gross,
Barbara Hillman, Harriet Hunter, Denise Jacobs, E.A. Korchnoy, Robert Maldonado, Jane Manoogian, Richard Manoogian, Cammie Naylor,
Patricia O'Grady, Julian Peabody, E. Gabriel Perle, Bernadette Quineri, Frederick Sammis, Tom Wilhelm, Robert Wormhoudt

and especially helicopter pilots:
Chuck Zanlunghi, Pete Zanlunghi, Bud Arnold and Chip Harper.

For their efforts in researching valuable historical data and translating this book into French,
I am most grateful to Josabeth Drucker and John Hughes.

Credits for historical and additional photography:
New-York Historical Society, pages: 4, 12A, 12C, 26, 46, 66, 84, 92, 126, 132; New York Public Library, pages: 16, 20, 32, 36, 40;
Museum of The City of New York, pages: 12B, 48, 78, 80, 90, 98, 130; Sports Illustrated, page 157 (A) Manny Millan (B) Neil Leifer;
Wide World Photos, pages: 8, 74, 76; Culver Pictures, page 114.

CAMERON and COMPANY

543 Howard Street   San Francisco, California 94105   (415) 777-5582

Library of Congress Catalog Number: 87-073037
Above New York ISBN 0-918684-42-0
© 1988 Robert W. Cameron and Company, Inc. All rights reserved.

First Edition, 1988
Second Printing, 1988
Third Printing, 1995
Fourth Printing, 1997
Fifth Printing, 1998

Book design by
JANE OLAUG KRISTIANSEN

Color processing by: Artform, Los Angeles; Duggal, New York; Modern Effects, San Francisco; New Lab, San Francisco and, Newell Color Lab, Los Angeles.
Typography by Minnowillo, San Francisco and Parker Smith. Camera work by Color Comp Graphics, San Francisco.
Color Separations by Dai Nippon
Printed In Singapore

New York is a city of vertical shafts. I lived on one growing up as a boy — fifteen stories above a back courtyard. On occasion, street musicians appeared far beneath my window. The practice was to wrap coin money in paper and drop it down that long cliff of grey brick. The musicians played glancing up from their accordions, violins, whatever, to dodge what came down for them, properly wary for what a youngster might be tempted to drop. I did that once — peeking over the sill, horrified once the paper waterbomb dropped from my fingers and cringing at the *splat* of it hitting the concrete; almost prayerfully relieved, I heard the strains of the Italian street song continuing uninterrupted. The musicians weren't shaken — such occurrences were apparently one of the occupational perils.

Writers covet their impressions of the city. That is one of mine. Christopher Morley called New York "the nation's thyroid gland"; Kurt Vonnegut, "The Skyscraper National Park," and O. Henry writes of the big city being like a "mother's knee," of all things, to which one who wanders can return. One of my favorite reactions is Truman Capote's — who, when driving over the last rise of the Long Island Expressway and seeing ahead the line of skyscrapers like a mirage against the sky, would inevitably exclaim, "Thar she blows!"

The greatest wonders of the place are, of course, what a poet has referred to as "the dreadful heights." No one visits New York without hoping to survey the city from above. The Observation Floor of the Empire State Building, which is the most famous of the sky-high aeries, one hundred and two stories up, has had nearly two million visitors a year since it opened in 1931. Robert Cameron, the master-photographer of this volume, has been up there, but only to survey the panorama, not to take pictures. His practice is to go higher, to look down on the Empire State Building and its environs and to take his picture from the domain of birds on the wing.

Cameron's tutelage in aerial photography came during the Second World War, when he spent four years working for the War Department. The post-hostilities helicopter with its ability to hover over a landscape constituted an important advance in aerial photography which Cameron was quick to take advantage of — now with practically a publishing monopoly on this sort of thing: *Above New York* is the eighth in the series. *Above Washington, Paris, London, San Francisco, Hawaii, Los Angeles* and *Yosemite* have sold over 2 million copies, and with the individual volumes each going through a number of printings.

The equipment Cameron uses is a Pentax 6x7cm — about four times as large as a regular 35mm camera. It's hand-held and attached to a gyro stabilizer — a device invented by a man named Kenyon who was head of research and development for Sperry Gyroscopes during World War II. Originally used at sea to steady a pair of binoculars, the officer-of-the-deck could watch for periscopes without getting queasy. Egg-shaped and weighing about ten pounds, the apparatus has two gyros encased in helium (one for pitch, the other for yaw) which emit a slight whine which Cameron can hear as he leans out the helicopter door to take his pictures. The loftiest photograph in the various 'Above' volumes was taken at 65,000 feet up over southern Oahu, not by Cameron but by a NASA camera in a U-2 reconnaissance plane. The lowest was snapped on the *ground* (of all places), also in the Hawaiian Islands, specifically in the mountains of West Maui where Cameron wanted to take a photograph of a slope of the rare silversword plants. To see this picture in *Above Hawaii* is almost a shock — as if Cameron, like Antaeus, has had to touch the earth on occasion to regain his powers.

Usually Cameron is hanging out the helicopter door. Suspended, he is harnessed securely, a piece of tape pasted over the release catch on the safety belt. On one occasion, photographing the start of the Grand Prix race in Long Beach, California

— the noise of the revving car motors the only sound from below Cameron has ever heard on the job save the thump of fireworks — he noticed as he leaned back after taking his final photograph that the end of the safety belt had become detached from the seat. He smiles as he recalls the pilot's pallid face when he showed him the unattached belt. "These days we check both ends of the safety belt," he told me. He smiled and asked if I'd like to take a helicopter ride with him above New York. He assured me there wouldn't be any leaning out of the open door.

We left from the 30th Street heliport on the West Side, the copter lifting and tilting out across the waters of the Hudson, and then rising to head down towards the lower harbor. We passed the Statue of Liberty. Our pilot Chuck Zanlunghi complained to us through the intercom earphones that he disapproved of the new torch. "Looks like a 1987 hood decoration on a 1927 car."

We headed back and rose over the Battery, past the World Trade Center, and up the spine of Manhattan. One is surprised at the number of architectural flourishes in the upper heights of the tallest buildings — filigreed stones, gold pyramids, copper greens, embroidered abutments, gargoyles — as if the architects thwarted in the lower reaches of their structures could only indulge their fancies up at the top. But the overriding sensation is that from above the city looks empty: so little moves that is discernible. All the descriptive adjectives about New York — "teeming," "bustling," "cacophonous," and so forth, are pertinent only at street level. From above they simply do not apply. One floats in the soft clatter of the helicopter. A pair of cormorants flew up the East River. A pigeon on dihedral wings ducked down into one of the great empty vaults below. The sense of desertion was heightened when we flew low over the commercial waterfronts, miles of the skeletal remains of docks, wharves, terminals, and warehouses to remind us how things have changed since the years of New York City as a great shipping port. It occurred to me that the real estate tycoons, clattering in their copters across such places, must wring their hands in the anticipation of turning these areas into residential waterfront properties.

We rose up from the river and started in over Manhattan. The deserted rooftops of Soho passed below. I spotted a few deck chairs. I asked, "Do you suppose there are any nudist colonies down there?" Cameron replied into my earphones that if that were a possibility he wouldn't find out until the photographs were enlarged. "The lens sees more than I do," he said.

The day was cloudy, bright with a high sky — not a good day for photographing, Cameron said. Seven o'clock on a summer evening is his favorite time to be aloft with his camera, the sun's rays filtering through the haze and dust, imbuing the landscape below in the soft gold that in his volumes is practically a Cameron trademark. He takes remarkably few pictures — three exposures to get what he wants, usually bracketing his target with a half stop each way . . . recalling his old friend, Ansel Adams' noted principle: "I'm a fly fisherman; I don't dynamite the stream."

We headed back to the heliport, the pilot taking us up 1500 feet so we could look up and down the entire length of Manhattan. The pilot said, "It's so beautiful I can't believe it's legal to be up here doing this."

I heard him in the earphones and nodded. Indeed, what a privilege, and so remarkably reflected in the photographs which follow.

"Pigeons in the grass alas." Gertrude Stein's curious line seemed to make a bit more sense. It suggested that a bird's proper element, especially an urban bird like a pigeon, was not in the grass, but on the wing — up there in Robert Cameron's splendid world!

— *George Plimpton*

ABOVE LOWER MANHATTAN in the 1920's shows an enormous amount of shipping activity in the harbor and at the piers. Now, most of the piers are gone, and those that remain serve ferries and occasional recreational sailboats. The skies over lower Manhattan, however, are far busier than they were when this biplane glided coolly over the city.

FROM THE BATTERY NORTH *(opposite)* the boxy towers of the last generation have made the skyline of lower Manhattan vastly less graceful than it was in the twenties and thirties – but its essential qualities still remain. The way in which this cluster of buildings seems almost to rise out of the water it as exhilarating as it always was; so, too, the sense that this agglomeration of buildings tempts chaos, but stops just short of it. Here we can see the shape of Manhattan laid out with almost as much clarity as a map – the narrow southern tip, the wider midsections, the second explosion of skyscrapers in midtown, and then the vista all the way up to the George Washington Bridge, on the left, in northern Manhattan.

TRINITY CHURCH GRAVEYARD at the foot of Wall Street, is one of the financial district's most treasured pieces of open space — a relic of a quieter, less built-up city, and far more pleasurable to spend a lunch hour in than most of the plazas of our own time. The space is tightly enclosed by office buildings like 111 Broadway (top), making it feel less like the rural churchyard it was in the 19th century and more like a vast outdoor room.

WALL STREET *(opposite)* — These buildings form the intense heart of the financial district. At right, just below the tower of the Brooklyn Bridge, is 70 Pine Street, designed by Clinton & Russell; in the center is the pyramid-topped 40 Wall Street, designed by H. Craig Severance and Yasuo Matsui. Both buildings are among the greatest of Manhattan's romantic towers from the early 30's. The glass slab at the top is the headquarters of the Chase Manhattan Bank — the building that launched the postwar boom of boxy skyscrapers in lower Manhattan.

LOWER MANHATTAN IN 1855 was more than a village, less than a metropolis. The spire of Trinity Church, then just nine years old, is visible in the lower center of this drawing; City Hall, built in 1811, is in the upper center. When City Hall was built, its rear was covered in inexpensive brownstone rather than lavish marble, for it was never expected that the city would move far enough north for City Hall's backside to be frequently seen.

LOWER MANHATTAN IN 1906, was beginning to take on its classic, Mont St. Michel-like profile. The greatest of its skyscrapers would not be constructed for several more years, but the center of the neighborhood was firmly established as the city's dense, high-rise business district, surrounded by the piers that brought the life of an active harbor to within a block or two of bankers' desks. This photograph was taken by J. H. Hare and is reputed to be the first aerial ever made of New York City.

1855

1906

LOWER MANHATTAN BY 1922, was denser still. It had acquired the Woolworth Building by Cass Gilbert at the upper right, the Gothic skyscraper finished in 1913 that was then the world's tallest; it lost that title to the Chrysler Building in 1930, but it remains among the most beautiful tall buildings ever constructed. Gilbert also designed the arch-topped tower at the far left.

1922

LOWER MANHATTAN *(opposite)* today shows how totally the scale has been transformed — where there was once a mix of small and medium-sized buildings, now all the towers of lower Manhattan seem gargantuan, and their boxy forms go all the way to the water's edge, crowding out the small-scale buildings that had served as a welcome counterpoint to the towers of an earlier generation. At the left are the biggest boxes of all, the twin towers of the World Trade Center, that are Manhattan's tallest buildings; to their left are the far livelier towers of the new World Financial Center, whose sculpted tops are an attempt to bring some romance back to the skyscraper form.

THE WORLD TRADE CENTER TOWERS are banal as architecture, but powerful as works of minimalist sculpture. Here, looking down into the space between them, we can see why. There is no sense of human scale here or, indeed, of human life in any form — but there is a staggering presence to this place nonetheless.

BATTERY PARK/WORLD TRADE CENTER *(opposite)* — The newest large-scale Manhattan development, and in many ways the best of the last generation, is Battery Park City, being built on landfill in the Hudson River. Its first phases are visible under construction on the left; in the foreground is more Battery Park City that will be filled in the coming years. The amiable, low building on the water, startlingly out of character amid the skyscrapers of lower Manhattan, is Pier A, the very southernmost pier on the Hudson River; the wood structure is a city landmark and is the boat house for the New York Harbor fireboats; there are plans to put a restaurant in it.

BATTERY PARK CITY — The towers of the World Financial Center, designed by Cesar Pelli, constitute the commercial core of the Battery Park City complex. Their stepped-back forms and decorative tops recall the shapes of more romantic towers from the years before World War II, here rendered in sleek, modern materials. An elegant riverfront promenade runs beside the residential section of Battery Park City to the right; this district is among the most successful new residential quarters to be built in New York in many years, designed as a conscious response to the stark, austere towers of most postwar developments. Instead of towers in open space, Battery Park City's residential areas have lower buildings set close together, with parks and open space inspired by those of traditional city neighborhoods.

THE OLD MUNICIPAL BUILDING, 1927, on the right, was completed in 1914 and designed by McKim, Mead & White; it is one of the nation's finest public works from the City Beautiful movement, when architects joined modern technology to Renaissance form in search of a civic grandeur suitable for the 20th Century. As serious, in their way, as efforts to achieve a noble degree of public monumentality were City Hall of 1811 in the foreground, the Tweed Courthouse of 1872, just behind it, and the Hall of Records, the mansard-roofed building just to the left of the Municipal Building. The aeroplane in the sky is a story in itself. The pilots performed a feat of endurance by staying airborne circling the city for two days to show that non-stop flight to Paris was possible. Shortly after they proved it, Lindbergh did it.

CIVIC CENTER TODAY *(opposite)* — Now, its great buildings remain, although the Tweed Courthouse was rescued by preservationists after the city tried to demolish it in the mid-1970's. But the order of the complex has been compromised by the construction of the Federal Building, the vulgar checkerboard tower, in the 1960's; it looms insensitively over the city's own buildings as well as the complex of courthouses at Foley Square just to the north of the city's administrative district. The Municipal Building proved that it is possible to erect a high-rise government building that enhances rather than detracts from the dignity of the buildings around it, but its lessons were lost on the Federal Building.

ELLIS ISLAND is in the foreground, with Lower Manhattan looming up behind it. It was the point of entry for most of America's immigrants in the late 19th and early 20th centuries. The island was , in effect, America's gatehouse, and many were turned away, their pain no doubt made more intense by the powerful presence of Manhattan so close across the water. The building in the center contains a great hall that is being converted into a museum of immigration, honoring the thousands who passed through the island.

THE STATUE OF LIBERTY *(opposite)* as it faces out to the harbor, appears almost to be floating at the edge of Manhattan, looking toward the city. The Woolworth Building is visible in silhouette to the right of the World Trade Center, and the Chrysler Building, way uptown, is the tiny silver sliver on the left.

GREENWICH VILLAGE IN 1923 north to midtown Manhattan. By now, the island is fully built-up and at fairly large scale, although the triumphant towers that marked the end of the period between the world wars were yet to come. The arch designed by Stanford White to commemorate George Washington is at the foot of Fifth Avenue in Washington Square, at the lower center of the photograph. The campanile-like tower of the Metropolitan Life Insurance Company, designed by Napoleon LeBrun and completed in 1909, is visible at 23rd Street to the right of center.

THE VISTA UP FIFTH AVENUE (opposite) now is not so different — the arch still anchors the southern tip of the street, and for the first mile or so, medium-sized buildings still predominate. By the mid-30's, though, it is a different matter — the Empire State Building at 34th Street announces the southern beginning of midtown Manhattan's high-rise business district with an unforgettable architectural climax, and from there northward it is a different city than it was in 1923.

THE LOWER EAST SIDE OF MANHATTAN
was never a well-to-do neighborhood and was for much of the late 19th and early 20th century the center of the city's immigrant Jewish community. In the foreground are public housing towers, built to replace blocks of tenements in the days when tearing down the old was considered the automatic first step in any neighborhood upgrading. To the left of center is Tompkins Square Park, the Central Park of the East Village neighborhood, the quarter that is now, more than any other, the city's center for young artists.

GREENWICH VILLAGE, *(opposite)* a beloved and historic quarter of small houses, shops, and vibrant street life. It is half a century since Greenwich Village has been the Bohemia it was once fabled for being in the 20's; today the occupants of Village houses are as likely to be bankers and lawyers as artists and writers. But this is still one of the city's most relaxed neighborhoods, and its low-rise character, now protected by city landmark designation, is its critical asset. In the early 1950's there were plans to redevelop the neighborhood with high-rise building. The victory of Greenwich Village's citizens over the planners was a crucial turning point in the postwar history of the city, for here the gospel that big new towers were better than the small, older buildings was challenged, and ultimately overturned.

THE WOOLWORTH BUILDING with its gentle, lilting Gothic form by Cass Gilbert, at the right, still presides over lower Broadway with the sumptuousness and graciousness it had when it opened in 1913. This is a story of rare stability in the fluid world of Manhattan real estate — the F.W. Woolworth Co. built the building, paid for it with $13.5 million in cash, has never put a mortgage on it, and has never moved its headquarters out of it. St. Paul's Chapel, a distinguished remnant of 18th-century New York, is in the center. It overlooks the base of the World Trade Center. One could not ask for a more striking demonstration of the passage of time; George Washington worshiped here.

SOUTH STREET SEAPORT (opposite) — These piers do not serve active shipping, but fulfill a different public purpose. They are part of the South Street Seaport Museum, where old vessels have been preserved in conjunction with a couple of blocks of old, low-rise waterfront architecture from the early 19th century. The red, gable-roofed pier at the north end is not a relic, however; it is new, and together with an inland pavilion it contains one of those new-style marketplaces of shops and restaurants that have been built to attract tourists, suburbanites and young professionals to older city centers.

PENNSYLVANIA STATION — A view across midtown Manhattan in the 30's, with the train yards in the foreground leading into Penn Station. Penn Station as a building is no more – this great McKim, Mead & White train station, completed in 1906 and modeled after the Baths of Caracalla in Rome, was torn down in 1963 to make way for the mediocre drum-shaped building that now houses Madison Square Garden, the city's sports arena. Trains now come and go from a cramped basement space underneath the Garden. Although it is only two decades old, the new Garden has been so roundly disliked - and is considered so inadequate – that plans are now afoot to replace it with a still newer Garden near the Hudson River. So the building that Penn Station was demolished for may itself be torn down. Alas, the plan is not to reerect the lost masterpiece, but to put two huge office towers on the site.

PARK AVENUE ABOVE GRAND CENTRAL was, until the 1950's, lined with uniform hotels and apartment houses that joined together to form an elegant boulevard. Now, the coherence of the old Park Avenue has given way to a free-for-all of office towers, with only the exclamation point of the Helmsley Building (originally the New York Central Building), the building with the elegant pyramid and cupola top constructed in 1929, remaining to give some flavor of what once was. The new pyramid-topped building on the right is Helmut Jahn's Park Avenue Tower, completed in 1987; to its right is one of the most celebrated — and controversial — buildings of the 1980's, Philip Johnson and John Burgee's headquarters for the American Telephone & Telegraph Corp., the building with the broken pediment "Chippendale" top.

PARK AVENUE SOUTH *(opposite)* begins at the The Pan Am Building, one of the city's largest, erected in 1963 over the railway tracks leading into Grand Central Terminal, the splendid Beaux-Arts structure that sits in front of it, facing Park Avenue to the south. If the Chrysler Building to the right, that exuberant piece of Fantasy Art Deco turned into a skyscraper, symbolizes the theatricality and flamboyance that are New York's best side, the Pan Am Building symbolizes the profiteering and preference for bigness over all else that is the city's worst side. In front and to the right of Pan Am is 101 Park Avenue by Eli Attia, a black glass building of abstract angles that represents a more recent trend toward picturesque abstraction as an alternative to the plain box. In the foreground are the low-rise blocks of Murray Hill, a comfortable and elegant residential neighborhood tightly surrounded by business districts.

THE SOUTHEAST CORNER OF CENTRAL PARK, where the Park meets the busiest section of midtown Manhattan, contains a landscape nearly as dense as that of the city around it. On the left is the recently renovated Zoo, whose new structures by the architect Roche are nearly complete in this view; on the right is the Wollman Rink, also renovated in the last few years, and in the center, the pond. At the corner, where the city meets the park, is Grand Army Plaza and the Pulitzer Fountain in front of the Plaza Hotel. In the early 1960's Huntington Hartford put forth a plan to build an immense cafe in the park just off Grand Army Plaza; it was greeted with a storm of protest. The backlash not only blocked the plan itself, but stood as the beginning of the current movement to keep the park landscape as simple and as close to Frederick Law Olmsted and Calvert Vaux's original design as possible.

THE EAST 50's *(opposite)* contain the blocks that have become the center of midtown Manhattan's business district in the last generation. Philip Johnson and John Burgee's A.T.&T. Building is just to the left of the center; when it was designed in 1978, the split-pediment top resembling a piece of Chippendale furniture caused something of a scandal, although by the time the building was completed in 1984, the re-use of historical form in new architecture had become common. To the right of A.T.&T. is the IBM Building designed by Edward Larrabee Barnes, far duller from this vantage point but possessing a fine, glass-enclosed public space at its base. To the right of IBM is the Fuller Building of 1929, by Walker & Gillette, a fine, faintly Aztec piece of Art Deco. In front of A.T.&T., meanwhile, is Park Avenue Tower by Helmut Jahn, the first New York building by a well-known architect of embellished, highly active towers in Chicago. Two other Jahn buildings are visible under construction in this view alone, one at top center, and the other at the bottom center.

1928 VIEW TOWARD QUEENSBORO BRIDGE — The eastern blocks of midtown Manhattan in 1928, when the city's business district had not yet spread out this far, and neither had much fashionable residential building. The steel trusses of the Queensboro Bridge, designed by Henry Hornbostel and completed in 1909, dominate the skyline. One exception to the general tone of the neighborhood in those days was the Beekman Tower Hotel (originally the Panhellenic Hotel), the handsomely sculpted tower by John Mead Howells that was finished in 1929. The rest of the area has the sort of casual, amiable mix of brownstones and small apartment buildings that once filled so much of Manhattan, and now has almost disappeared.

QUEENSBORO BRIDGE *(opposite)* — By the 1980's, there was almost nothing left of the small-scale residential neighborhood that had once filled the eastern blocks of midtown, and the bridge, though still a striking presence, hardly controls the skyline any longer. Office towers have taken over much of the district, the Empire State and the spectacularly spired Chrysler Building of 1930 by William Van Alen, New York's great monument of the Jazz Age, as the area's new centerpieces. High-rise apartment buildings now fill the northern and eastern sections of the neighborhood. The old Beekman Tower Hotel is still there, its suave form barely visible behind the triangular glass top of the 100 United Nations Plaza apartment tower.

THE NEW YORK PUBLIC LIBRARY, *(opposite)* completed in 1911 to the designs of Carrere & Hastings, is one of New York's great Beaux-Arts monuments — it manages to be both awe-inspiring and gracious, dignified and cheerful, in the way that the best American Beaux-Arts architecture could be. The ornate interior has recently been restored even as the library has modernized its internal systems, and the success of the restoration project stands as a reminder that classical architecture and computers can make a spendid harmony. Behind the library is Bryant Park, a rarity in New York: a formal square in the center of a business district. To the right of the library is 500 Fifth Avenue, a fine office tower from the late 1920's by Shreve, Lamb & Harmon, who were later to design the Empire State Building; visible on the left side of Bryant Park toward the top is the American-Standard Building (originally the American Radiator Building) of 1924 by Raymond Hood — one of the city's most celebrated early skyscrapers, the subject of a famous painting by Georgia O'Keeffe.

FIFTH AVENUE AND 57TH STREET, the intersection just to the left of center, is one of the city's most important retail locations. Tiffany & Company is in the restrained classical building on the right; Bergdorf Goodman in the building on the left. More interesting architecturally is the Crown Building, the 1925 skyscraper by Warren & Wetmore whose ornate top was recently restored and is elaborately lit each night. It is said to belong to Imelda Marcos. One block south on Fifth Avenue, next to Tiffany's, is Trump Tower, the multifaceted skyscraper of dark glass; it is something of a garish intrusion in this part of Fifth Avenue, and replaced the old Bonwit Teller store, an elegant limestone building that was a much more natural mate to Tiffany. Inside, Trump Tower contains a lavish, marble-lined shopping atrium and expensive condominiums for the super-rich. Behind it is the IBM Building, which contains a glass-enclosed public plaza at its base that is one of the city's most successful new public spaces.

MIDTOWN TOWARD CENTRAL PARK, 1925, shows a city of medium-sized, masonry buildings that surrounded Central Park. The Plaza Hotel is at the lower right corner of Central Park, and St. Thomas' Church and St. Patrick's Cathedral are visible below it on Fifth Avenue. Just opposite the spires of St. Patrick's is a site owned by Columbia University that in 1925 was full of low brownstones; by the early 1930's it would be redeveloped into the premier skyscraper grouping in the country—Rockefeller Center.

MIDTOWN BELOW CENTRAL PARK *(opposite)*—Everything is bigger now. The midtown business district has exploded into one of the densest concentrations of skyscrapers in the country. The RCA Building at Rockefeller Center is the dominant presence, and the finest of the very tall buildings architecturally here; many of the others are dull boxes from the postwar years. There is still energy and urbanity to midtown Manhattan's streets, but a strange kind of flatness to the crowded, jostling skyline of the late 1980's. The spires of St. Patrick's Cathedral are still visible, poking up in between a couple of boxy towers on Fifth Avenue. Even Central Park is different in this era—there is less of it, since the Metropolitan Museum, visible on the right side of the park just below the Reservoir, has more than doubled in size since 1925.

LINCOLN CENTER performing arts complex began in the 1950's as a slum clearance project — the blocks on which these marble buildings were erected once contained tenements that were among the city's worst. The best element of the center architecturally is the gracious and lively plaza surrounded by the three main buildings, the New York State Theater on the left, the Metropolitan Opera House in the middle and Avery Fisher Hall on the right. The architecture of the center's buildings is fairly timid classicism for the most part, but the impact of these structures on the life of the Upper West Side is undeniable. As evidence, look to the immense luxury apartment towers that have gone up across the street from Lincoln Center — uncomfortable intrusions on the skyline, but clear evidence of the economic health of what had once been a troubled neighborhood.

CENTRAL PARK SOUTH *(opposite)* — has one of the city's best skylines — anchored by the glorious form of Henry Hardenbergh's Plaza Hotel on the left and the spendid 1920's setback masses of the Hampshire House and Essex House hotels in the center. This street posseses the energy and theatricality of the classic image of Manhattan. Buildings of stone and the grass and trees of the park coexist in comfortable detente. Rising behind Central Park South, however, is a whole other city, vastly larger in scale and far less inviting — the immense black tower of 9 West 57th Street gives the Plaza a somewhat ominous backdrop, for example, with neither the graciousness nor the comfortable scale of Central Park South.

HOTEL PLAZA 1927 — At the end of the 1920's, the blocks of Fifth Avenue just below Central Park had only begun their transformation into a commercial district. The Plaza Hotel had been there since 1907, of course, and the Heckscher Building a couple of blocks south at 57th Street brought 26 stories of offices to the area in 1925. (It was renamed the Crown Building in our time.) But the vast, sprawling Vanderbilt mansion by Richard Morris Hunt still spanned the block between 56th and 57th Streets (it is visible between the Plaza and the Crown Building looking not exactly like the Renaissance chateau Hunt had hoped we would confuse it with, but close enough), and several other great mansions still stood on the avenue.

"THE PLAZA" TODAY *(opposite)* (Frank Lloyd Wright's favorite building in New York, and one of the few he did not design himself that he openly admired) is still at the southeast corner of Central Park, facing the elegant Pulitzer Fountain and Grand Army Plaza, and the Crown Building still holds the corner of 57th Street. But almost everything else in this refined quarter has changed since the earlier photograph. More than half a century ago Bergdorf Goodman replaced the Vanderbilt Mansion, the pinnacle-topped Sherry-Netherland Hotel long ago went up across Fifth Avenue from the Plaza, and two blocks to the north came the mansard-roofed Hotel Pierre. These were buildings that joined with the Plaza to make one of New York City's most urbane groupings - along with the Savoy Plaza Hotel, which was demolished in the 1960's to make way for the General Motors Building, the huge white slab designed by Edward Durell Stone that, perhaps more than any other new building in the area, sets a discordant note. (There are those New Yorkers who consider this site so critical that they view the replacement of the Savoy Plaza with the General Motors Building as a greater affront to the skyline than the construction of the World Trade Center.)

57TH STREET — Looking east on 57th Street from Eighth Avenue, where the Central Park Place apartment tower, designed by Davis, Brody & Associates, is under construction. From here, this looks like a canyon of cars — in truth, 57th Street is one of New York's most urbane boulevards, with a splendid array of shops and art galleries that make it, like all great city streets, more amenable to the pedestrian than the motorist.

42ND STREET — There is something astonishing about the way New York streets run right to the river; they are canyons that seem to run on forever, until the water stops them. This view looks east on 42nd Street from the old McGraw-Hill Building by Raymond Hood on the right, a triumph of the International Style in New York dating from 1932, past Times Square, where New York Newsday had put up an advertising sign on the old Times Tower, the building made famous three-quarters of a century ago by The New York Times. The Times itself is still in the neighborhood, in the building with a vaguely Gothic pyramidal top at the far left.

BROADWAY as it runs through Times Square, the heart of the theater district, is increasingly coming to look like the rest of midtown Manhattan: the office towers are taking over. The city has made efforts to preserve the legitimate theaters that are the neighborhood's great land-marks, but the tone of this quarter has still changed dramatically as skyscrapers take over the sites in between the old theaters, as well as sites previously occupied by old movie palaces, which are not protected. John Portman's Marriott Marquis Hotel is the immense, double-slabbed structure on the right: if all the construction presently planned for this area goes ahead, it will look not like the vast intruder it appears to be today but like a medium-sized old friend. The oddly shaped tower at the top is One Times Square, a crude 1960's makeover of one of New York's most beloved, if eccentric, buildings, the Times Tower of 1904.

THE EMPIRE STATE BUILDING — In early afternoon — or so we can surmise by looking at its great shadow, aiming to the north. The building may function as a great sundial from there, but from the ground it is one of the city's most beloved icons, a tower that has become not only the image of New York around the world, but in many ways a kind of Platonic image of the skyscraper.

PARK AVENUE TO MIDTOWN – This is Manhattan with an image of order it does not always have – the central spine is Park Avenue, the East Side's great boulevard, seen here from 96th Street looking south toward the skyscrapers of midtown. The Helmsley Building (originally the New York Central Building) stands astride Park Avenue at 46th Street as it has since 1929. Behind it is the Pan Am Building, and to the left is the spire of the Chrysler Building and the sleek boxy form of Citicorp Center, while the Empire State Building balances the skyline vista on the right. Then heading further south, are the lower blocks of the 20's, Greenwich Village, and SoHo, below which the skyline explodes upward again into the cacophony of skyscrapers that represents the financial district.

MADISON AVENUE is the heart of the residential Upper East Side, the blocks of ornate townhouses and solid, somber apartment buildings between Central Park and Park Avenue. Madison Avenue, the city's most elegant shopping street, is at its center. What this view shows clearly is how much lower, on the average, buildings are here than in surrounding districts. The reason is the designation of the Upper East Side as an Historic Commission, which has kept this area's remarkable mix of small and medium-sized buildings largely intact and free from the development pressures that have turned so much of Manhattan into a celebration of gigantism.

LINDBERGH'S RETURN TO NEW YORK, 1927, shows the harbor and the skyline at their best: strong, self-assured, sumptuously rich, and wildly exuberant. Charles Lindbergh returned to New York after his flight across the Atlantic as one of the great heroes of the modern age — but the event in this picture was more than a lot of tooting of tugboat horns. It is important to keep in mind that New York itself in those years was a symbol of modernity and energy; the city was celebrating itself, reveling in its own power and glory, as much as it was honoring Lindbergh.

THE HARBOR *(opposite)* — It is a bigger city now, less graceful in its skyline thanks mainly to the presence of the World Trade Center's twin towers, which render once-substantial buildings trivial, almost toylike. The quieter harbor is not only a reflection of the absence of a particular event like the Lindbergh welcome — it is also a reminder that there is much less going on in New York harbor all the time now, as shipping has declined or, in many cases, moved to less expensive ports.

It is the **SUMMER OF 1865** and this is how artist John Bachmann portrayed "Lake Belvedere, how Olmsted completed his vision of Grand Park."

CENTRAL PARK FROM THE NORTH *(opposite)* — The edge of Harlem is in the foreground in this view of Central Park looking down toward midtown Manhattan's skyline. It is striking to notice how much of the upper end of the park is covered by water or ice. (On this day the wind-chill factor in an open-doored helicopter at 1500 feet was minus 28 degrees Farenheit.)

CENTRAL PARK'S lushness stands in stunning contrast to the hard edges of Fifth Avenue's apartment buildings. But while the presence of large buildings may destroy the illusion of being in a total wilderness that the park's designers, Frederick Law Olmsted and Calvert Vaux, had hoped for, the interplay between buildings and nature creates a splendid visual counterpoint. The buildings of Fifth Avenue form an even, well-mannered wall; it would be far less pleasant without the trees, but in an odd way, the trees would be far less interesting without the wall of buildings.

THE METROPOLITAN MUSEUM OF ART *(opposite)* – When the trustees of the museum won permission to locate their buildings in Central Park late in the 19th century, they thought they were bringing the art museum to a tranquil edge of the city. But the city grew densely around the museum, and the museum itself has expanded continuously over the last century. The sections facing the park were designed by Kevin Roche, John Dinkeloo Associates and have been constructed over the last 12 years; they are of glass and limestone, and stand in deliberate contrast to the classical, limestone architecture of Richard Morris Hunt and McKim, Mead & White's front sections on Fifth Avenue.

CENTRAL PARK (opposite) is glimpsed here from the West Side, over the shoulders of two of the great landmarks of the Central Park West skyline: the San Remo apartments, the twin-towered structure on the left, and the Majestic apartments, the twin-towered structure just to the right of center. They were both finished in 1930, and are quite similar within. But architect Emery Roth chose to garb the San Remo in a lavish Italian Renaissance style, while Irwin Chanin wanted the Majestic to be an overt symbol of modernity, and sheathed it in Art Moderne brickwork. In between is the single tower of Roth's Oliver Cromwell Hotel and to its left, barely visible behind the bland white-brick apartment tower, is the legendary Dakota apartments by Henry J. Hardenbergh.

CENTRAL PARK'S great reservoir, its 1.66-mile circumferential track, New York's most popular jogging site, fills much of the east side of Central Park in the blocks above 86th Street. Visible facing the reservoir on Fifth Avenue is the spiral of Frank Lloyd Wright's Guggenheim Museum of 1959, among New York's most beloved modern buildings; in the blocks to its left remain several distinguished mansions that have been converted into museums, including the old Andrew Carnegie Mansion, now the Cooper-Hewitt Museum, which sits in its own garden at 91st Street, two blocks to the north of the Guggenheim. The immense and somber tower at the far left is the Annenberg Building of Mount Sinai Hospital, completed in 1976.

THE TAVERN ON THE GREEN was created in the 1930's by expanding an old building that had housed sheep in the park's early days. Today there is little sympathy for putting commercial facilities into the park, but what is there is generally permitted to remain, and in 1976, the restaurateur Warner LeRoy won permission to take over the lease for Tavern on the Green and expanded it still more, turning the tavern into an immense, shimmering glass fantasy amid the trees. Visible on Central Park West just beyond the Tavern on the Green is 55 Central Park West by Schwartz & Gross, a 1929 apartment building in the Art Moderne style that has a pleasing quirk: its brickwork is shaded gradually from dark at the bottom to light at the top, which the architects hoped would give the impression that the building was always in sunshine.

RIVERSIDE PARK *(opposite)* – It does have the Henry Hudson Parkway running through it, but even so, Riverside Park is one of Manhattan's treasures – designed originally by Frederick Law Olmsted beginning in 1873 and reconstructed in 1937 to the designs of Clinton F. Lloyd, the park is both a refuge in itself and a miles-long perch from which to view the broad Hudson River. The undulating form of Riverside Drive is a welcome counterpoint to the grid of most of Manhattan; visible toward the top of the picture is the Soldiers and Sailors Monument of 1902, a columned tower based on the Choragic Monument of Lysicrates in Athens. The boat basin and round automobile interchange at 79th Street were part of the 1937 reconstruction, which was an outgrowth of the decision to bury the New York Central freight tracks that had run through the park for generations.

THE CENTRAL PARK BANDSHELL was long the site of summer concerts, which moved to Lincoln Center's outdoor Damrosch park in the late 1960's. Now, the bandshell is used for special events, but there is some discussion of removing it altogether and replacing it with a more modest facility in keeping with the present preference to minimize large-scale intrusions into the park landscape.

THE LOEB BOATHOUSE on the lake in Central Park is both headquarters for rowboats and a pleasant, low-key eatery. Like many buildings in the park, it has been expanded and restored in a manner consistent with the park's master plan, which guards the natural landscape designed by Frederick Law Olmsted and Calvert Vaux.

THE SHEEP MEADOW (opposite) is a great open lawn on the west side of the park that was for years in the 60's the site of summer concerts. Protectors of the park's landscape succeeded in moving them to a more durable section of the park farther north, freeing the meadow for "quiet activities" — picnicking, resting, kite-flying, or anything else that keeps the stress level down.

THE BETHESDA FOUNTAIN and set of terraces at the south end of the lake, designed by Calvert Vaux and Jacob Wrey Mould, were among the few formal and elaborate intrusions in Olmsted & Vaux's otherwise rustic Central Park landscape. Restored, the fountain with the lake as a backdrop is one of the city's most intriguing vistas: at once urban and rural.

THE ZOO (opposite) has been in Central Park since the 1920's, just behind the Arsenal, the 19th century building that predates the park itself and serves as headquarters for the city's parks department. The zoo is being completely rebuilt, designed by Kevin Roche.

EAST RIVER PARK AND THE WILLIAMSBURG BRIDGE — Many of the tenements of the Lower East Side have been replaced with brick towers standing in open space, most of which lack the neighborhood quality of their predecessors. Much of the riverfront in this area has been turned into parkland, however, which is a boon to this densely populated section. The Williamsburg Bridge was completed in 1903, the second span over the East River.

UNION SQUARE *(opposite)* was for years New York's Hyde Park, the favorite spot for rallies and public speaking by radicals of every stripe. It now houses a very different population: on the weekends, the square is the scene of a farmers' market, with trucks of fresh produce lined up all around it. Union Square has ridden the up, down and up again fortunes of its 14th Street neighborhood, and right now sparkles with a recent reconstruction. At the upper left is Zeckendorf Towers, a four-towered complex of apartments and offices designed by Davis, Brody & Associates that confirms the neighborhood's gentrification.

THE WOLLMAN SKATING RINK in Central Park was recently rebuilt by real-estate developer Donald Trump who took over the project after the city stumbled.

CENTRAL PARK RESERVOIR *(opposite)* partially iced-up in winter: the city appears cold and utterly calm, yet nothing keeps joggers, with a wind chill factor of minus 15, away from their path around the reservoir.

THE MUSEUM OF MODERN ART SCULPTURE GARDEN has been one of the most civilized oases in midtown Manhattan for nearly half a century, it has been redesigned several times — most recently after the museum's tower addition by Cesar Pelli was completed — but its basic form has remained intact. This is a truly urban garden, a mix of masonry, water, plantings and sculpture, and it proves that one does not need acres and acres to create a sense of serenity.

MADISON SQUARE *(opposite)* marks the intersection of Broadway and Fifth Avenue, and it has three of the city's finest tall buildings on its periphery. The greatest is the Flatiron Building, the triangular tower on the right designed by Daniel Burnham & Co. and completed in 1902, one of the city's most celebrated skyscrapers for more than three-quarters of a century. Taller, and nearly as beloved, is Napoleon LeBrun's Metropolitan Life Insurance Tower, modeled after the campanile of St. Mark's in Venice; after its completion in 1909 it was the world's tallest building for four years, until the Woolworth Building was finished. Beside the Metropolitan tower is the insurance company's later building, its current headquarters, a sumptuously massed limestone mountain designed by Harvey Wiley Corbett and finished in 1932.

SARA DELANO ROOSEVELT PARK, 1940, was one of the few bits of open space in the crowded Lower East Side, almost entirely a neighborhood of tenements. At the bottom: the monumental entrance to the Manhattan Bridge by Carrere & Hastings, an unlikely piece of public classicism.

SARA DELANO ROOSEVELT PARK (opposite) remains largely as it was. The ethnic mix of the Lower East Side has changed — it is now heavily Hispanic, where it was once almost entirely Jewish — but the physical fabric of the quarter has not shifted as dramatically. Chinatown is to the lower left of this picture, and the large tower in the lower left corner is called Confucius Towers, built to house the area's rapidly expanding Chinese population.

TOMPKINS SQUARE PARK is the one green space in the East Village, as the northern sections of the Lower East Side are known. Now filling with young artists, architects, writers and musicians who can no longer afford Greenwich Village, Soho or much of anyplace else in Manhattan, this is still a troubled neighborhood and it is thus a troubled park. But the presence of a square of green nonetheless provides critical relief and breathing space to a part of New York that, despite the relative paucity of very tall buildings, still can feel excessively dense and closed in. Walking the streets here one rarely has the sense that the East River is as close as it appears here, from the air.

STUYVESANT SQUARE *(opposite)* is an unusual New York square, for it is bisected by a street, Second Avenue, yet has a fairly tranquil air nonetheless. It was once an elegant residential quarter, and its neighborhood has begun to gentrify once again. Beth Israel Hospital overwhelms the east and north side of the square (the top and the left of this photograph), but the best architecture is on the west side: St. George's Church, a great Romanesque mass from 1856 that was where J.P. Morgan worshiped, and beside it the Friends Meeting House and Seminary, a spare, strong gem of 1860.

MARCUS GARVEY PARK, formerly Mount Morris Park, interrupts Fifth Avenue between 120th and 124th Streets. It is rocky and awkward in size — too big to be a square, too small to be a major park — and in recent years the city has filled it with well-meaning, but ultimately heavy-handed recreational buildings. This is among central Harlem's few relatively high pieces of land, which is why it has at its centerpiece a cast-iron tower, built in 1856 as a location for watching out for fires.

GRAMERCY PARK *(opposite)* is New York's most English square, and in almost every way its most pleasing. It is private — it can be entered only with a key, and only owners of property on the square have keys — but its quiet calm is easily enjoyed from outside the fence. Lexington Avenue stops at the point where it intersects 21st Street and the park, as if to symbolize the extent to which uptown tensions halt at the park's gates. Every outdoor urban space is a kind of room, but Gramercy Park is particularly roomlike, for the buildings that line the park make such fine walls: on the south side, for example, are the National Arts Club and the Players Club, while 34 Gramercy Park, one of the city's oldest cooperative apartment buildings, holds sway over the East Side.

THE CIRCLE LINE is not the Intrepid or the Normandie – it feels more like the subway when you are on it – but the Circle Line is a true New York institution. These little red and green-striped boats have been going 'round Manhattan island for what seems like generations; it is a trip that reminds everyone, tourists and cognescenti alike, what is continually forgotten: that Manhattan really is an island, and that the city looks different from the water.

FERRIES FROM NEW JERSEY – One encouraging sign in the last few years has been a revival of interest in the waterfront, both as a source of recreation and as a functioning part of the city. Ferries across the Hudson River between New Jersey and New York died off in the 1950's, but have been reborn on a limited basis. Here is one of the first of the new generation, leaving from a pier in Weehawken and headed across the river to midtown Manhattan.

AN OUTBOUND OCEAN LINER *(opposite)* cruising the waters around Manhattan Island at dusk, when the extraordinary light gives off an aura both mystical and exhilarating.

THE NORMANDIE, among the most beautiful liners ever built, caught fire and capsized in New York Harbor during conversion for military use in 1942, it was a devastating event — not so much for the war effort, which could survive without the Normandie, as for the finality with which it marked the end of the era of sophisticated, Art Moderne design in ocean liners that the Normandie so utterly epitomized.

THE INTREPID *(opposite)* — Now, the aircraft carrier Intrepid sits in the Hudson River, as a permanent floating museum. It honors not only American military might of World War II, but the lost glories of New York Harbor: a visit to the Intrepid is the first time many New York area children ever see, let alone enter, a ship of this size.

OCEAN LINERS IN 1957 — There was once a time when each day's New York Times contained a column called "Shipping/Mails" that listed the major passsenger liners and cargo ships arriving and leaving that day — for so heavy was the harbor traffic that some kind of scorecard was needed. Not that it was a record, but on this day, September third, 9,350 passengers debarked from seven liners, left to right, Britannic, Queen Mary, Mauretania, Flandre, Olympia, United States, and Independence. The assemblage of liners was a spectacular visual event, covering eight blocks bounded by 44th and 52nd Streets as it joined with the skyscrapers to create a vision of 20th-century urban possibility.

OCEAN LINERS TODAY (opposite) — Now, passenger ship traffic has slowed to a trickle of cruise ships. The decline came just after the city and the Port of New York Authority, in their infinite wisdom, invested significant sums in creating a new and modern passenger ship terminal to replace aging piers on the Hudson. In this view the terminal serves some of its rare customers.

FREIGHTYARDS 1929 — From the 19th century well through the midpoint of the 20th, the riverfront was seen as an industrial resource, not as a scenic or recreational place, by virtually every American city, including New York. These freightyards and piers epitomize the tendency to remove living space from the waterfront and turn it over to industry.

THE JAVITS CONVENTION CENTER *(opposite)* section of the waterfront has not been reclaimed totally from industrial use — there are still trainyards on the left, for example, although this site has been discussed as a possible new location for the city's arena, Madison Square Garden. On the right is the Jacob Javits Convention Center, the I.M. Pei-designed glass palazzo that is among the nation's largest convention centers — and one of the few to display significant architectural aspirations. The two brown structures on either side of the Hudson are "breather buildings" to ventilate the Lincoln Tunnel.

COLUMBUS CIRCLE IN 1920, at the southwest corner of Central Park, looked much more like a circle than it does today — whatever else can be said about the old buildings that surrounded it, at least their shapes reflected and thus enhanced the shape of this unusual intersection. Now only the two largest buildings on the left remain. The excavation for the old General Motors Building at 1775 Broadway is visible one block off the circle just left of the center of the photograph; at bottom right, the columned structure is the old Century Theater, a lavish building designed by Carrere & Hastings that would be demolished by the end of the decade.

COLUMBUS CIRCLE *(opposite)* — The buildings that were the largest things around the circle in 1920 are now the smallest. The newest generation for the most part ignores the geometry of the circle; buildings like the New York Coliseum in the center and the Gulf + Western Building on the right could be anywhere. The Coliseum has been made obsolete by the new Jacob K. Javits Convention Center, and is slated for demolition and replacement by a large office and apartment tower. In 1987, controversy over the immense size of the proposed new building led to abandonment of the original plans, and now the final form of the project is uncertain.

THE UPPER WEST SIDE'S *(opposite)* landscape is as clear as a map from here; on the right is Central Park West, lined with large apartment buildings such as the Majestic on the lower right and the Dakota, Langham, and San Remo to its left; townhouses along the side streets, and at the left, along Columbus Avenue, tenement-type apartment buildings with retail shops on the ground floor. Wider side streets, such as those facing the American Museum of Natural History near the top of this picture, break the pattern with their large apartment buildings, and here and there a new tower deviates from this traditional urban pattern as well.

CENTRAL PARK WEST — A slice of the Central Park West skyline with four of the finest apartment houses ever erected. On the left, between 71st and 72nd Streets, is Irwin Chanin's Majestic Apartments of 1930, a twin-towered essay in Art Moderne. To its right is the legendary Dakota, by Henry Janeway Hardenbergh, finished in 1884, one of the first truly grand apartment houses and the building that did more than any other to popularize the idea of apartment living in New York. Just north of the Dakota is the Langham, by Clinton & Russell, of 1905, and beside the Langham is another twin-towered building of 1930, the San Remo by Emery Roth, whose Renaissance-inspired towers are one of the skyline's most elegant punctuation marks.

THE MUSEUM OF NATURAL HISTORY SITE IN 1894 was Manhattan Square, a four-block long chunk of land off Central Park West between 77th and 81st Streets set aside for the American Museum of Natural History. In this view, taken well before the turn of the century, the museum's first wing sits rather forlornly in the midst of this open space, and the surrounding blocks are only beginning to be developed.

THE AMERICAN MUSEUM OF NATURAL HISTORY *(opposite)* has grown like the city itself — continuously and to a size its founders barely imagined. The Romanesque wings fronting on west 77th Street (in the center of this view) were designed by J. Cleveland Cady, who also designed the old Metropolitan Opera House. The classical entrance on Central Park West (in the right of this view), which is a memorial to Theodore Roosevelt, was the work of architect John Russell Pope. At top right is Emery Roth's Beresford Apartments of 1928, one of the city's grandest classically-inspired apartment houses; just left of center is the Park Belvedere, a new building by Frank Williams that is the first luxury tower to be built on Upper Columbus Avenue. At bottom center is the Natural History Museum's small but venerable neighbor, the New-York Historical Society, the museum whose classical building was designed by York & Sawyer and later expanded by Walker & Gillette.

PANORAMAS OF
CENTRAL PARK WEST

CITY COLLEGE CAMPUS *(opposite)* — Old and new do not blend particularly gracefully at the campus of the City College of New York off 138th Street. The curving Gothic building, designed by George B. Post and completed in 1905, could be the centerpiece of a rural campus — which City College once was — and is an absolutely splendid work of collegiate Gothic architecture, with considerably more flair than most such buildings. Unfortunately, new additions to the campus are less successful, and tend to be among the harsher examples of postwar modernism, with little effort made to respect the bucolic ambience that was once this campus' most notable quality.

TRINITY CEMETERY in the center, is the large burial ground at 155th Street started in the mid-19th century by Trinity Church of Wall Street. The cemetery adjacent to the downtown church no longer had room for its elite parishioners so the remains of such personages as John Jacob Astor were barged up river to 155th street to this new burial plot. Within the cemetery is Bertram Grosvenor Goodhue's Church of the Intercession built in 1914, a splendid piece of Gothic massing by one of the 20th century's true masters of Gothic composition, and a church that, thanks to its setting, has more of the feel of a true country church than almost any in Manhattan. On the left is one of New York's strangest places — Audubon Terrace, a cluster of four Beaux-Arts buildings that was intended to function as a kind of American Acropolis. These classical temples are rather small, almost hesistant more than monumental. Visible at top, across the Harlem River in the Bronx, is Yankee Stadium.

MORNINGSIDE HEIGHTS — The original McKim, Mead & White-designed grouping at the campus of Columbia University, upper left, was complete by the time this photograph was taken, probably early in this century. The Cathedral of St. John the Divine, in the center, had only its Romanesque crossing finished — the great Gothic nave was barely begun. Morningside Park is on the right, and at the bottom, the elevated train tracks of the Ninth Avenue El are visible running up Columbus Avenue and turning right at 110th Street.

THE CATHEDRAL OF ST. JOHN THE DIVINE *(opposite)* on Amsterdam Avenue at 112th Street was known for years as St. John the Unfinished — but no more. In the early 1980's the cathedral resumed construction of its Gothic edifice, the south tower of which can be seen slowly rising. The project is particularly unusual in that the cathedral is training members of the community, many of whom had been in need of work, in the reviving art of stonecutting, making this a community service venture as well as an architectural one. The cathedral began in 1892 as a Romanesque design by Heins & LaFarge; in 1911, Ralph Adams Cram, the nation's most ardent Gothicist, took over and designed the nave in Gothic. It is Cram's plans that are providing the basis for the current construction. It is by the way , the largest Gothic cathedral in the world.

COLUMBIA UNIVERSITY here clearly shows the formal order of Charles McKim's plan; the great Low Library of 1897 in the center, and academic buildings tightly arranged around it with a huge open lawn and field as the campus' centerpiece. Not many years after this photograph was taken in 1922, the large field gave way to Columbia's new Butler Library; Low Library was retained as the campus' symbolic and ceremonial building, but Butler took over the role of the university's working library.

THE CAMPUS OF COLUMBIA UNIVERSITY *(opposite)* at 116th Street and Broadway is dense, but by the standards of New York it has plenty of open space. Its centerpiece is the sumptuous, domed Low Library; the smaller domed structure just to the right of Low is Howell & Stokes's St. Paul's Chapel, an intriguing mix of Byzantine and Renaissance elements. Most of the campus was designed according to a master plan that called for a dense arrangement of similar Italian Renaissance classroom buildings.

RIVERSIDE CHURCH AND GRANT'S TOMB *(opposite)* — Riverside Church on Riverside Drive at 120th Street was another gift of the Rockefeller family to New York City. Designed by Allen & Collens, Henry C. Pelton and Burnham Hoyt and completed in 1930, this is a solid and clean Gothic building, with none of the deep mystery of great European Gothic architecture, or even of its neighbor a few blocks to the south, the Cathedral of St. John the Divine. Riverside Church is more matter-of-fact, and it is hard not to look at it and conclude that by 1930 the passion had gone out of the Gothic Revival. The passion has not gone out of Riverside's congregation, however, which has always been among the city's most socially concerned and responsible. To the left, within Riverside Park, is the very dry and very formal classical monument designed in 1897 by John H. Duncan to house the bodies of General Ulysses S. Grant and his wife.

THE CLOISTERS — John D. Rockefeller Jr. underwrote the building of the Cloisters, a medieval museum that is a division of the Metropolitan Museum of Art, in Fort Tryon Park in Upper Manhattan in 1938. The complex is actually a series of medieval cloisters from France and Spain, dismantled and reassembled by architect Charles Collens around a new tower which Collens designed as a centerpiece. There are splendid views to and across the Hudson River, startling in the illusion of distance from the city that they create, since Rockefeller had the rare foresight to purchase considerable amounts of land on the Palisades across the Hudson River in New Jersey and restrict development there.

COLUMBIA PRESBYTERIAN HOSPITAL, in the foreground, is one of the city's great medical institutions. Its main buildings were designed by James Gamble Rogers in the 1930's, and after years of unsympathetic additions by other architects, are now receiving a new wing, visible under construction on the left, that will be in keeping with the original architecture. The hospital sits in a dense, overcrowded section of Washington Heights, and from most blocks here there is little sense of the spectacular visual drama of the neighborhood's great monument — the George Washington Bridge.

CENTRAL HARLEM *(opposite)* — Seventh Avenue, renamed Adam Clayton Powell Jr. Boulevard, runs up through the center of Harlem. The large building in the middle is a New York City office building, constructed in 1973.

THE HARLEM RIVER here in 1937 is spanned by two steel bridges, the Broadway at bottom and the just-opened Henry Hudson at top.

THE HARLEM RIVER *(opposite)* — The northern tip of Manhattan Island on the left, joined by the arch of the Henry Hudson Bridge to the Riverdale section of the Bronx on the right. The Palisades, the great cliffs on the New Jersey side of the Hudson River, are at the top. In the center, near the point of Manhattan, is Baker Field, Columbia University's football stadium. A veterans' hospital in the Bronx is in the foreground.

There are times when traffic on the water in **NEW YORK HARBOR** resembles traffic on the land in Manhattan Streets – this is a view of the stretch between Governor's Island and the Statue of Liberty which at a busy moment can approach the nautical equivalent of gridlock.

THE STATUE OF LIBERTY looks out to the entrance to New York Harbor, joining with the Verrazano Narrows Bridge to give the city's entry by water a monumental presence. In the foreground, on Liberty Island, are the renovated grounds and parkland surrounding the statue, re-done for Liberty's centennial in 1986.

STATEN ISLAND FERRY TERMINAL (opposite) – A Staten Island Ferry churns away from its pier and toward Staten Island as night falls on the East River.

THE WATERSIDE PLAZA apartments, built on a platform in the East River at 25th Street, were designed by Davis, Brody & Associates and completed in 1974. They represent a striking attempt to create quality housing in a city that has seen little of it in recent years. The United Nations International School is the low building in front of Waterside; Bellevue Hospital is the large boxy mass behind the four Waterside towers. The bend in the Manhattan coastline at Waterside makes for a good point to view the city's skyline, with the Empire State Building at its center.

THE WORLD TRADE CENTER (opposite) – Only a helicopter could create this extraordinary view – a combination of a dramatic angle and foreshortened perspective brings together the roof of one of the World Trade Center towers and lower Manhattan's greatest monument, the Brooklyn Bridge. They are actually in opposite sides of lower Manhattan, but they come together here in a vista of startling power.

THE UNITED NATIONS HEADQUARTERS is on the East River, its slab set against the midtown Manhattan skyline. Long ago the site of the United Nations contained slaughterhouses, which is why the apartments in the complex called Tudor City, at the far left of the picture, had no windows facing the river: residents would not have wanted to see or smell their neighbor. In the years since the United Nations complex was finished in 1952, the neighborhood has exploded with prosperity and a plethora of new apartment and office towers.

THE BROOKLYN BRIDGE *(opposite)* looks most spectacular when it is set against the background of the lower Manhattan skyline — when both bridge and skyscrapers are seen together, they join together to make a vista of staggering visual power: this is New York.

THE QUEENSBORO BRIDGE, a virtual tunnel of metal trusswork in the air designed by Henry Hornbostel and finished in 1909, crosses over Roosevelt Island to connect midtown Manhattan to the borough of Queens. The little red tram car flies through the air next to the bridge, giving Roosevelt Island residents an alternate means of transportation, one of the best rides New York has ever offered.

ROOSEVELT ISLAND *(opposite)* in the middle of the East River, spanned by the Queensboro Bridge, was first called Blackwell's Island, and was long known as Welfare Island because of its large number of hospitals, many of which served the indigent. Now, the island contains an impressive new community developed under the aegis of the New York State Urban Development Corporation in the early 1970s. At the southern tip of the island is the Delacorte Geyser, a vast fountain donated to the city by philanthropist George Delacorte.

NEW YORK HOSPITAL, the great white mass completed in 1933 and designed by Coolidge, Shepley, Bulfinch & Abbott, recalls the drawings of Hugh Ferriss, the artist-architect who envisioned skyscrapers rising up like mountains. To its south are the red-roofed buildings of Rockefeller University, a distinguished institution for medical research; all around the hospital are apartment towers of the rapidly expanding Upper East Side neighborhood. Most of the tallest were built just in the last few years — when the hospital was finished, it stood alone as the only tall building along the riverfront.

THE BEEKMAN PLACE *(opposite)* district's blocks of the 50's between Second Avenue and the East River have maintained their residential character despite significant development pressures in the last few years. Some parts of this district, like the elegant and discreet two-block long Beekman Place, are true enclaves. But throughout the district many blocks of brownstones have been preserved, and they mix fairly well with the large buildings in the area, such as the two United Nations Plaza apartments towers in the upper right, among the few New York City apartment buildings which owe a design debt to the architecture of Mies van der Rohe. Several venerable towers from the 20's are visible here: the Beekman Tower Hotel by John Mead Howells at 49th Street and First Avenue, just to the left of the United Nations Plaza apartments; One Beekman Place, right on the river to the left of U.N. Plaza; and, in the upper left, at the far east end of East 52nd Street, River House, the 1931 tower that once had its own private yacht mooring, and 40 years after it was removed to make way for the East River Drive is still among the most sumptuous luxury apartment buildings in the city.

THE TRIBORO BRIDGE, which connects Manhattan, the Bronx and Queens, begins with the truss structure in the center, then snakes around to become the suspension bridge at the top. The arched structure on the left near the top is the Hell Gate Bridge, a great railroad bridge completed in 1917 to make possible a connection between the trains coming into Pennsylvania Station and the tracks to the north and east.

YANKEE STADIUM *(opposite)* in the foreground was elaborately rebuilt by the City of New York in exchange for a commitment from the New York Yankees to continue playing baseball in their longtime home in the Bronx. In the center of the view is the Harlem River, and below it, Manhattan, with Fifth Avenue in the center running south past Central Park.

GRACIE MANSION is the official residence of New York's mayors. It sits in Carl Schurz Park on East End Avenue, a serene upper-middle-class neighborhood far from the hectic pace of midtown Manhattan. The park has an unusual riverfront promenade, with the Franklin Delano Roosevelt Drive slipped underneath, properly keeping automobile traffic far from pedestrians and parkgoers.

SIX BRIDGES — The Triboro Bridge's suspension span parallels Hell Gate railroad bridge to leap across Hell Gate and join Randall's Island to Queens. In the distance: the Bronx Whitestone Bridge and the Throgs Neck Bridge, both suspension bridges joining outlying parts of Queens to the Bronx. There are six bridges all told in the photograph. Count them.

THE GRAND CONCOURSE is the Bronx's great central artery, a wide boulevard that runs north-south along one of the three ridges that make the Bronx's topography more unusual than that of the rest of New York. To the right, railroad tracks parallel the Grand Concourse.

THE BRONX (opposite) in the 1930's and 1940's was an immense and stable middle-class area, and the concourse was lined with six-story Art Deco apartment buildings that were the reward for those who could work their way out of Manhattan's slums. In the 1960's the concourse area itself began to decline, but there are recent and encouraging signs of revival.

THE HENRY HUDSON BRIDGE from Manhattan and The Henry Hudson Parkway form the main entrance to the Spuyten Duyvil, and further north, to the Riverdale-on-the-Hudson and Fieldston sections of the Bronx, which until the late 1950's was a true suburb within the city. High-rise apartment buildings have altered its physical makeup to a large extent, but there are still substantial clusters of sumptuous mansions and greenery.

RIVERDALE *(opposite)* the way its residents like to see it — as a gracious, private neighborhood of handsome homes looking over the Hudson River. And indeed, from here, the high-rise apartments that have filled so much of Riverdale are barely visible: it is not difficult to sit on the lawn of one of these houses and believe you are a hundred miles from Manhattan.

VAN CORTLANDT PARK with its great open spaces, a stunning and lush contrast to the density with which so much of the rest of the borough of the Bronx is built up, contain almost every kind of sport – in this case, a game of cricket.

VAN CORTLANDT PARK *(opposite)* is the largest park in the Bronx: large enough for its own golf course. The Riverdale section is off to the right, along the Hudson River; the rest of the Bronx is to the left.

THE NEW YORK BOTANICAL GARDEN is the proper name for the City's greatest public gardens, which happen to be in the Bronx. The lavish conservatory with its glass dome was recently restored. On the right is a portion of the campus of Fordham University; at the top, off in the distance, is the immense high-rise project called Co-op City.

C.C.N.Y. LEHMAN COLLEGE/KINGSBRIDGE ARMORY *(opposite)* — In the center of this view of the Kingsbridge section of the Bronx is Lehman College, a division of the City University of New York; its campus is a mix of 1930's traditionalism and 1960's and 70's modernism. The neighborhood's real architectural climax is at the bottom — the Kingsbridge Armory, completed in 1912 and designed by Pilcher & Tachau. It has been called the largest armory in the world by the A.I.A. Guide to New York, but whether or not this is so, the armory is surely the city's most remarkable mix of medieval romanticism and 20th-century monumental scale.

THE NEW YORK ZOOLOGICAL SOCIETY is known to the world as the Bronx Zoo. At the center are its main buildings; the rounded structure at bottom is the Lila Acheson Wallace World of Birds, one of the first zoo buildings anywhere to present animals in an "environment," outside of conventional cages.

BRONX ZOO *(opposite)* — The most astonishing thing about the Bronx Zoo from the air is what an immense park it is — this truly is a sea of green in the midst of the Bronx. In the winter, when the leaves are off the trees, it is easier to see the zoo's architecture, especially its original grouping of buildings by Heins & LaFarge, opened in 1899, that are arranged in a formal, Beaux-Arts axial pattern. The Elephant House, the centerpiece, is just to the left of the center of this view.

THE COAST OF LONG ISLAND SOUND takes on the trappings of luxury as the Bronx gives way to Westchester County. In the foreground is the Glen Island Casino, a grand mansion facing the water. From here to Rhode Island, the coast is an intriguing combination of small inlets, peninsulas, and tiny islands.

CITY ISLAND *(opposite)* is technically part of the Bronx, but like that other place with official Bronx address but very different sense of itself, Riverdale, it is worlds away. City Island is a small, low-key community on the water, with a happily disproportionate share of boats. In the distance is Orchard Beach, a public work constructed by Robert Moses in 1936.

CONEY ISLAND, in 1910, in Brooklyn was once the city's great seaside amusement center. All of its architecture was fanciful, but nothing equalled its building in the shape of an elephant.

CONEY ISLAND TODAY *(opposite)* has no more elephants, and the beachfront amusement parks are quieter than they once were, but Coney Island remains. Now the great roller coasters are the high points of its skyline.

BENSONHURST, recently famed for being the site of much of the filming of "Saturday Night Fever" and for being where Barbra Streisand and Dom DeLuise 'came from,' is a quiet part of Brooklyn on Gravsesend Bay. Drier Offerman Park, in the foreground, is where Little League plays hardball and grown-ups play softball. Also visible are the Marine Basin Marina and the Excelsior Yacht Club.

BROOKLYN HEIGHTS *(opposite)* is one of the most prized residential neighborhoods outside of Manhattan. Its blocks are filled with splendid townhouses and gracious, medium-sized apartment buildings. And there is a waterfront promenade with spectacular views of Manhattan and the great bridge.

GRAND ARMY PLAZA, 1928, is the formal entrance to Prospect Park, Brooklyn's great Olmsted and Vaux-designed park. At the center is the Soldiers and Sailors Memorial Arch, designed by John H. Duncan and completed in 1892.

GRAND ARMY PLAZA TODAY *(opposite)* — The arch still holds sway over the center of Grand Army Plaza, but a major site at the corner of Prospect Park's entrance has been taken over by the Brooklyn Public Library, a rather banal attempt in 1941 to merge the simplicity of modernism with the monumental order of classicism. On the left is the Brooklyn Museum, designed in 1897 by McKim, Mead & White.

THE BROOKLYN BRIDGE, finished in 1883, was for at least the first decade of its existence, the tallest thing on either side of the East River: its towers were, in a sense, the city's first skyscrapers.

THE BROOKLYN BRIDGE *(opposite)* no longer towers over its surroundings, at least not on the Manhattan side, and neither does its less graceful mate, the Manhattan Bridge, completed in 1909.

QUEENS BOULEVARD is the Wilshire Boulevard of this part of New York — a long, wide street that runs through every type of neighborhood, and functions as a kind of linear city for much of its length. The unusual round structure near the top is a branch of Macy's department store, designed by Skidmore, Owings & Merrill in 1965. There is parking around the perimeter of the circle, with shopping floors in the middle.

FOREST HILLS GARDENS *(opposite)* in Queens is one of New York's real treasures, a utopian suburban community designed by Grosvenor Atterbury in 1913 and sponsored by the Russell Sage Foundation. It is a picturesque neighborhood of winding streets, leafy trees and gracious, red-roofed houses.

THE JFK AIRPORT CHAPELS epitomize the gimmicky kind of thinking that was behind the design of Kennedy Airport—the area in the center of this picture is named Tri-Faith Chapels Plaza. It does, of course, contain chapels for the three major western faiths, which have always seemed rather forlorn in the midst of a sea of parked cars.

THE INTERNATIONAL ARRIVALS BUILD-ING of John F. Kennedy Airport was designed by Skidmore, Owings & Merrill and completed in 1957. In its day, it was the *sine qua non* of airports—but after more than three decades of intense use, the facility seems small, cramped and utterly lacking in the majesty a major gateway should possess.

SATCHMO ARMSTRONG STADIUM AND TENNIS CENTER (*opposite*)—The United States Open Tennis Tournament was played in Forest Hills tennis stadium for many, many years. In the late 1970's, however, the tournament moved to this new facility in Flushing Meadow Park in the center of Queens, ideal in all ways but one: the noise of jet planes frequently interrupts play. Being directly under one of LaGuardia's flight paths also makes getting clearance to fly a helicopter near the stadium very difficult.

THE TWA TERMINAL is the most ambitious work of air terminal architecture at the vast John F. Kennedy International Airport. It was completed in 1962 to the designs of Eero Saarinen. Here, at last, an architect tried to design a building that would be as serious a work of architecture as the great train stations, yet would express the special nature of air travel. Saarinen's structure of swooping concrete vaults now appears a bit dated, and has not been cared for by TWA as well as one might have hoped — but it is still Kennedy Airport's masterpiece.

THE BRITISH AIRWAYS TERMINAL at JFK is a structure of harsh concrete, perhaps designed to give departing travelers a foretaste of the architecture they will soon experience at Heathrow in London. Parked on the left is a British Airways supersonic Concorde.

LAGUARDIA AIRPORT, New York City's smaller, closer-in airport, also in Queens, honors one of the city's great mayors, Fiorello LaGuardia. The airport was built for the World's Fair of 1939 with the splendid round Art Deco structure of the Marine Terminal as its first building. The terminal originally serviced the great flying boats: now it is just an adjunct terminal for conventional aircraft. In the distance, connecting outlying Queens to the Bronx are the Bronx Whitestone Bridge, and, behind it, the Throgs Neck Bridge.

THE STATEN ISLAND FERRY is coming Into St. George. "We were very tired, we were very merry, we had gone back and forth all night on the ferry," wrote Edna St. Vincent Millay, and if you do not want to stay on it all night, the Staten Island Ferry is still one of the great experiences in New York. It is no longer a nickel — inflation has brought this rambling, leisurely 20-minute boat ride up to the massive fare of a quarter — but it is much as ever the best way to see the skyline of lower Manhattan and get a feeling for the geography of the harbor. From the ferry you see how much New York is a water city, and how gloriously Manhattan seems to float, like a vision, on the bay. In this view the ferry is approaching St. George, the port of Staten Island, at bottom.

THE VERRAZANO-NARROWS BRIDGE is New York's longest suspension bridge, and it was the last design of Othmar H. Ammann, the engineer who had designed the George Washington Bridge in his younger days. There is, alas, no pedestrian walk on this bridge, which joins Staten Island to the Bay Ridge section of Brooklyn, so its graceful form is best admired from a boat in the harbor — or from a helicopter.

STATEN ISLAND *(opposite)* is the oddest borough of New York — not only is it more a suburb in feeling, it is geographically closer to central New Jersey than to most of New York City. Indeed, it was only with the completion of the Verrazano-Narrows Bridge in 1965 that Staten Island had any direct connection to another part of New York City at all. The bridge goes over the Narrows, the entrance to New York Harbor; its opening set off a land rush in Staten Island, with acres of undeveloped land turning into tract houses and small apartment developments.

NEWARK AIRPORT is the oldest of the metropolitan area's three major airports, although it is also in a sense the newest — it was entirely rebuilt by the Port Authority of New York and New Jersey in the early 1970's. The skyline of lower Manhattan is visible in the distance in the upper left, and the Verrazano-Narrows Bridge connecting Brooklyn to Staten Island is in the upper right.

THE GEORGE WASHINGTON BRIDGE, (opposite) designed by Othmar H. Ammann and completed in 1931, remains New York's most stirring 20th-century bridge. In this view, looking toward New York, the George Washington Bridge Bus Terminal designed by the Italian engineer Pier Luigi Nervi in 1963 straddles the bridge approach roads. Below the New York tower is the little red lighthouse, which inspired the children's book of that title.

143

PALISADES INTERSTATE PARK, NEW JERSEY — Tightly nestled together above the Palisades in New Jersey, across the Hudson River from Yonkers (From the old Dutch word for aristocrats, 'De Jonkers'), are three golf courses.

PALISADES INTERSTATE PARK, NEW JERSEY *(opposite)* — A little further south in this vast area reserved as a parkland, the autumn colors reflect the afternoon sunlight.

YANKEE STADIUM is not as picturesque as it was before its renovation — but it looks a lot better with a crowd than empty. Today is April 14, 1987, opening day, and it's raining, but the stadium is sold-out. Everyone has an assigned seat in a sell-out. (Those not in their seats are waiting for the rain to let-up and play to resume.) The sun finally came out and the stadium filled to its 55,000 capacity. Yanks over Indians 11-3.

THE OLD WORLD'S FAIR SITE *(opposite)* is now Flushing Meadow Park. The framework globe in the middle was the symbol of the 1964 fair; the more inventive Trylon and Perisphere that were the logotype of the 1939 fair were torn down. On the right are the towers of the New York State Pavilion by Philip Johnson, one of the best buildings at the 1964 fair, which happily has been preserved — although with no new function, it sits empty and derelict. The annual Queens County Fair is currently in progress on this site.

THE EASTER PARADE was made famous by Irving Berlin, but even before his time it was traditional to stroll on Fifth Avenue after Easter Sunday church services. The Easter Parade is less a parade than a mingle, but that would not have given Berlin as neat a lyric.

THE TRADITIONAL HERO'S WELCOME involves a slow and triumphant procession up Fifth Avenue in midtown as here the crew of the 12-meter sailboat, "Stars and Stripes," having just won the America's Cup back from Australia, is being saluted with ticker-tape and confetti.

THE ANNUAL GAY PARADE is a big event bringing thousand of spectators from the entire metropolitan area to line 5th Avenue. The New York Public Library on the left continues to function as usual and the sun bathers on the rooftop across the street seem indifferent to the spectacle.

MACY'S THANKSGIVING PARADE is perhaps the most beloved of all New York's parades. It is surely the one that transforms the cityscape most dramatically: the great balloons, which include huge blowups of such cartoon characters as Garfield, Donald Duck, Woody Woodpecker and Superman, are almost like Claes Oldenburg sculptures. They are monumentally scaled pieces of magic; each passes by for a wonderful moment, and then they float on downtown.

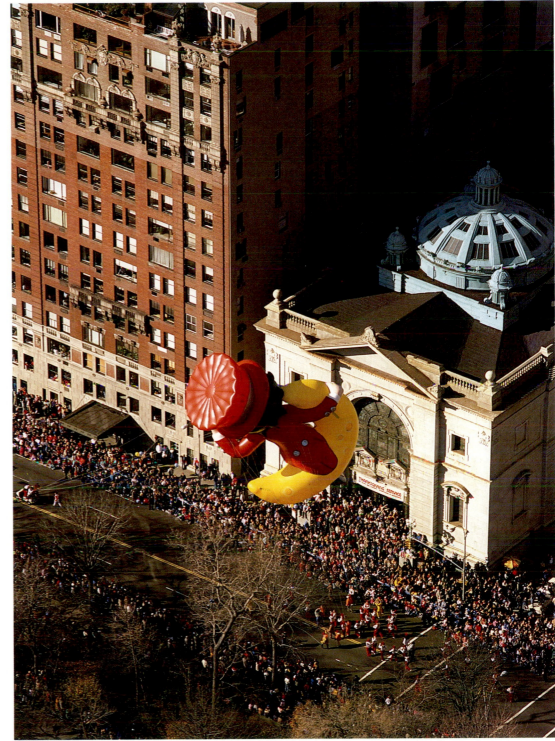

THE EMPIRE STATE BUILDING'S lighting in the 1970's, designed by the sign and lighting consultant Douglas Leigh, has been one of the seminal events of the New York skyline, for it has inspired the owners of many other buildings to light their tower tops, too. Here are the colors of New York's beloved METS. And on the right, the RCA Building is now entirely flood-lit from top to bottom.

SHEA STADIUM, (opposite) here at the opening of the 1986 World Series, saw the New York Mets eventually win from the Boston Red Sox in a dramatic final game.

THE BELMONT RACETRACK is in Elmont, New York, just across the line separating the borough of Queens from suburban Nassau County, Long Island. The Belmont Stakes every Spring is the track's most famous race, the third jewel of the triple crown of racing. Alysheba was the favorite, having won the Derby and the Preakness, but on the day this picture was taken over 64,000 watched Bet Twice run away from the field.

THE MEADOWLANDS SPORTS COMPLEX, built in the swamps of New Jersey, has a football stadium, an arena, and a racetrack for horses, so why not a place for auto racing? This is a Formula 1 racetrack, with a 1.68-mile course that threads its way through the parking lots and access roads of the complex – not as simple a route as the Indianapolis 500, but much more interesting. About 35,000 spectators can be accommodated.

THE BRENDAN BYRNE ARENA is in the center of this view during a night baseball game and the Meadowlands Racetrack, also in operation, is beyond. Nearby, out of the picture is Giants Stadium, now the home of the football team that still calls itself, officially, the New York Giants.

THE NEW YORK CITY MARATHON is such an institution that it is difficult to believe it has been going on only since 1970 (1976 in its prersent form). It may have the most spectacular start of any marathon anywhere: runners (about 22,000 in 1987) congregate on the Staten Island side of the Verrazano-Narrows Bridge, and at the gun cross the bridge over New York Harbor. The 26.2-mile route covers all five boroughs of the city, and takes runners through such diverse neighborhoods as the lush brownstone precincts of Park Slope and Fort Greene in Brooklyn, the Hassidic neighborhood of Williamsburg, also in Brooklyn, and the industrial neighborhood gentrifying into artists' quarters of Long Island City in Queens. The route crosses the Harlem River into the Bronx, then back into Manhattan, ending at Tavern on the Green in Central Park.

GOOD NIGHT NEW YORK

The most remarkable thing about seeing New York from a helicopter is that it is not like seeing New York from an airplane. The city is not far off, a distant panorama, to be absorbed only in great swaths of vista, as it is from an airplane. From within a helicopter New York breaks up into a million little pieces, and you feel as if you are a part of each of them. You have the intimate connection with the city that is possessed by the walker on the street, you feel the texture of the buildings as you pass them, and the fact that it is the tops that you are responding to rather than the bottoms matters not at all. Indeed, it makes the view all the more extraordinary, since there is a glorious sense of tasting forbidden fruit to experiece hovering beside the Chrysler Building or moving past the Woolworth Building. You do not believe that you were ever supposed to see these rich architectural details up so close. Moving through midtown Manhattan in Bob Cameron's helicopter is like floating through the upper reaches of Chartres, or levitating in the Sistine Chapel.

New York's architecture has always been one part pragmatic, one part wildly flamboyant, and for all Bob Cameron's photography does to celebrate the city's greatest skyscrapers, the view from the helicopter does not hide broader truths about the city's buildings. The banality of most postwar skyscrapers is as evident from 2,000 feet as from street level. The only difference is the magical silence that descends on all of these buildings from way above; it confers on the dreary boxes the grace of softness, while it lets the inventive forms of the city's greater towers emerge with all the more strength.

The other thing a view from above does is remind you clearly of how little of New York City is built up to the height of midtown and lower Manhattan, of how much of the city sprawls low rather than rises high. Much of New York's five boroughs remain parkland, of which Central Park is but a medium-sized example, and still more of the city consists of rows and rows of townhouses or single-family dwellings. From a helicopter this city is the capital of an empire, as spectacular and as awesome as ever, and it is also a place like any other.

– P.G.

Page 2

ORCHARD BEACH AND CITY ISLAND, eastern edge of the Bronx's Pelham Bay Park, was reopened in 1936 after a WPA facelift under the jurisdiction of Robert Moses's Department of Parks, at that time a haven for the victims of the first Black Monday in 1929. The spacious entry terrace encloses a cafeteria. City Island was originally a salt-making center, then a busy oyster-fishing area. Yacht building has long been in evidence there, and City Island's "Intrepid" won the 1968 America's Cup. D.W. Griffith brought his filmmakers to City Island and the Keystone Kops shot some memorable footage on Fordham Street. The island is still as much New England as New York City, and attracts anyone with a yearning for good seafood.

Page 3

CONEY ISLAND was once a truly magical part of New York, the beach at the end of Brooklyn that was in every sense the city's party ground. The boardwalk was only the beginning: the great amusement parks next to the sea were the really extraordinary thing, the places where all of New York's tendencies toward architectural fantasy got their most complete expression. Steeplechase Park, Luna Park and Dreamland were the main amusement parks, but only tiny portions of Coney's fantasy structures remain, such as the Parachute Jump and the great roller coaster, the Cyclone. Much of Coney has given way to subsidized housing, and what remains is but a tawdry echo of the glamour that once was.

Page 4

SAINT PATRICK'S 1922 – James Renwick's rather formal and dry Gothic church finished in 1888 – presided grandly over midtown Manhattan. Its slender spires were this neighborhood's skyscrapers, and even though the church always did have the feeling of a building that wished it were out in the country rather than in the middle of a city, the presence of low buildings around it gave the cathedral at least some sense of openness.

Page 5

SAINT PATRICK'S CATHEDRAL is barely visible now among the office towers of midtown. Its closest neighbor is the splendid Rockefeller Center complex, most of which was built in the late 1930's; the RCA Building, Rockefeller Center's finest tower, is the tall slab with its front edges gently sculpted back, above and just to the left of the cathedral spires. The slant-roof top of Citicorp Center is visible at the bottom, and at the lower left, the exquisite Gothic pinnacle of the GE Building, designed by Cross & Cross and finished in 1931, one of the few towers in Manhattan to bring St. Patrick's Gothic style up to skyscraper scale.